With his first work *Bump* due to be published in 2024, Andrew J. William credits the beguiling charm of his Shropshire home for much of his inspiration. Nestled amidst the natural beauty of the Shropshire Hills the environment William now finds himself in is highly conducive to creativity – far removed from his boyhood years growing up in Luton, Bedfordshire.

William continues to work on his wider writing project fantasy series *Rainbow Web Tales,* promising a collection of adventures and stories, all intertwined, that explore his fascination with rainbows and magical worlds, whilst reliving his childhood in Luton during the 1970s.

William shares his time between country life, working as a training manager, and spending time with his partner planning new adventures together.

ANDREW J. WILLIAM

BUMP

A LITTLE HORSE'S TALE

AUSTIN MACAULEY PUBLISHERS™
LONDON • CAMBRIDGE • NEW YORK • SHARJAH

A CIP catalogue record for this title is available from the British Library.

ISBN 9781398499263 (Paperback)
ISBN 9781398499270 (ePub e-book)

www.austinmacauley.com

First Published 2024
Austin Macauley Publishers Ltd®
1 Canada Square
Canary Wharf
London
E14 5AA

Acknowledgement and thanks:

To Mum and Dad for believing in me all those years ago and funding my first writing course, and to my family and friends who have read my work and believed in me.

To Amelia, my amazing goddaughter, and her sister Chloe, who were the inspiration for Bump.

Finally to my wonderful partner who has been my editor, my muse, and the driving force behind me finally embarking on this journey as we write our own next chapter in the adventure called life.

Thank you 'Debs' – you are proof that true love can come true!

Mere Green Stable Yard
Ashton Clayton, near Cayderwood, Somerset

The little white horse with the floppy black forelock always looked forward to the weekends; Saturday was her favourite day because there were always lots of different people coming and going at the yard, which in turn meant that there would be plenty of children there too, all getting on with their jobs and chores and looking after all the other horses: mucking out, sweeping up, brushing, cleaning, feeding – there was always plenty that needed doing.

She knew that the children giggled at her because of her small size and her funny look. They called her 'Bump' because of the lump on her forehead, but she was sure that they didn't mean any harm by it. She tried to keep it covered as best she could beneath her floppy forelock, but *she* knew it was there, even if the other horses and the humans couldn't see it.

Bump had a little home all to herself just next to where the muck and the used straw was dumped, a short walk away from the main stable block. She wasn't with the other horses because no-one *really* owned her, although she didn't understand why that was.

Bump could remember being with her mother and their family one day when she was a very little foal; she had been happily munching hay by the side of the road when her owner had tied her to the fence, hitched up their home onto the back of their two big shire horses called Flynn and Clyde and had then just ridden off, her mother tied to the back of the caravan galloping along behind looking back at her in anguish, neighing frantically as they disappeared around the bend, never to be seen again.

She remembered trying to pull away from the fence to go with them, but the rope had been tied so tightly she couldn't. She had whinnied out in desperation, but it had been no use.

Fortunately, a kind lady called Mrs Mullen had found her later that day, and before she knew it, Bump had ended up at the Mere Green Stable Yard in her own special little stable.

The stable could have been a lot worse, she guessed. It was comfortable, and she always had enough food. When it rained her stable leaked a bit, but she just stayed away from that part and slept in the other corner until it dried out again.

The only thing that she really wished for was that one day, she would have a little friend of her own to come and brush her and talk to her. That was her favourite magical wish, and she thought about it every day as she watched all the other horses getting looked after and loved by their children and their families.

Bump knew that she was different in other ways too.

None of the other horses could understand what the children were saying, but she could. The grown-ups weren't so easy to fathom, but they didn't really matter. It was the younger girls and boys that she loved to listen to, although sometimes she didn't approve of what she heard – like when Milly Tucker told Gracie Meadows how she'd stolen some of Sally Maynard's carrots, or when Natalie Wilder had told her friend Lillie that she had borrowed Heather Wilson's broom without asking her, and had 'accidentally' kept it.

Once she had heard Delilah Oliver shouting at her horse Matrix, and she didn't like that one bit. The girls could also be really nasty about some of their classmates at school, and Bump always moved to the back of her stable when she could hear stuff that she didn't want to hear.

Most of the children were much more pleasant than that though.

Bump loved to stand behind her lower stable door with her head resting on its top edge and watch all the comings and goings in the yard. When she thought that someone was coming over towards her stable her ears would prick up and she would swish her tail in excitement; usually though they were just going to empty their wheelbarrows onto the used straw pile, and although she watched them and willed them to come over, very few of the children ever did.

Her favourite person was a little girl called Cassie.

Cassie wasn't at the yard every week, but when she was, she always made sure that she came over to see Bump to say hello. She usually had a treat too – either an apple, a carrot or a handful of hay. Cassie would pull over a step and stand in front of the stable door so that she could stroke Bump's poll and tickle her under her chin, which Bump loved, although Cassie would never stroke her forehead.

Bump always wondered about that, and it made her think that she must look strange or even ugly, but she couldn't help it. How she looked was how she was: she just wanted to be a normal little horse who just happened to have a slightly peculiar lump on her forehead.

The one person that she really *didn't* like was Veronica Mullen, Mrs Mullen's daughter. It was Veronica who had said that Bump had to sleep in the old stable, because 'why should they give a perfectly good stable to such a strange little pony when they could get full rent for it from someone with a proper horse'... Hearing that made Bump feel really sad, but she never showed it. She just hoped even more that she would be a 'proper' horse herself one day. It made her angry too because she wasn't a pony! She might have been little, but she was still a proper horse!

A few times every week, Bump was let out of her stable to go and join the other horses in the fields. She loved these times. Last month all the horses had been very excited because the piebald mare called Thelma had given birth to a beautiful new foal called Sky, so named because the sky was perfectly blue the day that she had been born. Bump thought that Sky was ace, and she'd even come over to say hello to her one day before Thelma had become a little too protective and told Sky to 'go and play with the other horses please dear, there's a good foal'.

Bump usually kept herself to herself in the fields, but it was still lovely to be out and about. Some of the other horses would chat to her, but most would just stay in their own little groups and whinny on about how good their lives were, their ears twitching as if deep in gossip about the strange little horse that they all had to endure.

If it rained, Mrs Mullen would usually put one of the old horse coats over her if there was one spare, which helped, although it was invariably a little bit too big.

She did have some friends though, and two best equine friends in particular.

'Shire' had a bit of a limp and therefore couldn't walk around too much, so he was always in the first field. He was quite funny and loved to do impressions of the other horses when they weren't looking.

'Bodo' had a funny fat lip and tended to dribble a lot. All three got teased by the other horses, but they became close friends *because* they were different; to them they were merely more special. They helped to look after each other too, especially when one of them needed it, just as proper friends always should. A lot of the other horses would neigh and bray and snigger about them behind their backs, but the two boys never seemed to mind, and they always looked out for Bump if some of the bigger horses got a little bit too nasty.

Bump never let on about how sad it made her feel when the other horses called her 'shorty bump face' or 'bobblehead'. She just wanted to fit in, and not sound ungrateful for being allowed to stay at the Mere Green Stables. Okay she wished that she was more like the other horses sometimes, but she wasn't, and that was that. So she just got on with her life as best she could and tried not to worry about it too much.

Little could Bump imagine, therefore, how much her world was about to change forever.

It had been the most horrible and miserable Thursday that anyone could have ever imagined with rain, hail, wind and thunder. Bump hated the thunder because it really scared her. The stable was leaking even more that day due to the incessant rain, and when one of the stablehands finally came over and shut her stable door entirely, it meant that she couldn't even look out across to the other horses like she usually did. All in all, therefore, Bump felt thoroughly downhearted that particular day.

It was early afternoon by the time that the rain finally stopped, and then a little while later when one of the yard staff called Maria came over and opened Bump's top door for her and threw some fresh hay into her stable. She immediately trotted over to the door and popped her head outside, just like she always did. Bump looked around, her ears twitching and alert as the yard slowly began to spring into life. The weather still seemed a bit gloomy but she didn't mind, she was just glad to be able to see out into the world again.

She looked across towards stable number 7 which was the last stable in the block closest to where she lived. Number 7 used to belong to a horse call Kingdom, but she remembered seeing Kingdom being led into a horsebox and driven away a week or so before, and the stable had been empty ever since. Now though there was a flurry of activity going on in Kingdom's old home; it was all very exciting.

She watched as a posh new horsebox pulled up and a man and a woman got out. The man unbolted the side of the trailer and gently lowered the gate to the ground. Then the woman went in, and a few minutes later emerged leading a beautiful dark grey gelding down the slatted tailgate. She watched in anticipation as number 7 suddenly pinged into light and the new horse was led inside. The lower section of the stable door closed and the horse

soon came over to look out from his new home. He looked across the yard, and Bump was sure that he looked directly at her for a single fleeting moment. That was enough though. *WOW, who's he*, she thought out loud and blushed as only a mare could blush.

Gradually the afternoon began to fade into more gloom, the sky continuing to grumble like a stroppy child. Bump was just thinking of settling down when she saw a young shape in the gloom coming towards her. At first she assumed that it was just one of the stable hands coming over to check that she was okay.

As the figure drew closer, however, Bump realised that she didn't know the person; it was a little girl with dark brown hair and glasses wearing a shirt and white denim skirt. Not the usual yard attire, Bump thought, but she looked like she was a very happy child all the same.

The little girl slowed down as she got closer, looking intently into Bump's stable. There was no light, but the floodlights that illuminated the dressage yard opposite cast enough of a glow to enable each to see the other in a little more detail. The young girl edged closer still and then stopped, and they just stared at one another for a moment.

Bump pricked up her ears, her eyes brimming with excitement at the thought of a new friend to talk to. However the young girl just smiled, turned, and ran back towards the stables. *Typical,* Bump sighed, just another girl who had come to make fun of her. She lifted her head wearily back inside her stable and plodded over to the far side where she planned to lay down and go to sleep for the night.

Ten minutes later though she heard a hushed commotion outside.

Bump pricked up her ears again, keen to know what was going on. She stood up and edged herself towards the stable door, straining her little head to try and see what was happening. What she saw really surprised her.

The young girl was back, and this time she had company.

“Look Amelia, I told you, it’s so cute!” Bump heard the younger girl say to another girl that now accompanied her.

“Aww it is, I can’t believe it! Hello, little horsey!”

Bump could understand what the two girls were saying because of the magic, but she still couldn’t believe what she was hearing.

“What do you think its name is?” asked Amelia, her eyes wide with excitement; the little horse thought out loud ‘*my name is Bump*’ as she swished her tail, but she knew full well that they wouldn’t be able to understand her.

“I don’t know, I guess it depends whether it is a boy or a girl?” *I’m a girl silly!* Bump smiled to herself and let out a small whinny.

“I think it looks more like a girl,” said Amelia, “because she’s adorable, much cuter than a boy would be!” to which both girls laughed. *That’s right! I am a girl and yeah, I guess I am rather cute!* Bump thought and with that she fluttered her mane and pricked her ears forward even more, keen to hear what the girls would say next.

“Look there’s a step, pull it over Chloe, let’s have a proper look,” said Amelia, her voice full of glee.

Chloe fetched the metal step and stood on it. They were both soon leaning on the top of the lower stable door eyeball to eyeball with the cute little horse – and they were now as close as they needed to be for what happened next.

So you must be new around here, Bump thought to herself, still a little bit reluctant to get too close just in case it was another trick. Some of the girls at the stables were always playing mean tricks on her.

“Hello!” chirped Chloe. “Yes, we are new to the area; we have a horse called Moonshine and we have just moved him into his new stable, that’s why we’re here. He lives in number 7 over there.” With which she pointed across the yard to where the new horse was.

Bump looked at the girl in amazement. *Can you hear what I*

am thinking? She thought with a bemused look on her long face.

"Of course I can!" replied Chloe, who looked at Amelia and smiled.

"So can I!" said Amelia, and then in unison the two girls looked at each other, and then back at the little white horse before proclaiming:

"We both can! We can both hear what you are thinking!"

With that Bump looked alarmed – then surprised, and then amazed.

Wow, I've never met anyone that can hear my thoughts before!

Bump was so thrilled that she started to tap the floor of her stable with her left hoof as she edged closer to the door.

"Yeah, that's what Moonshine said to us too," said Amelia. "He was really nervous when we first got him, but once he knew that he could talk to us, he knew that he could tell us if there was something wrong, or if he needed anything."

Amelia and Chloe had discovered that they had the magic one day whilst talking to their old cat Charlie; ever since then they had been able to speak to all of their pets as long as they were close enough so that no one else could hear. They never knew how the magic worked, just that it did.

I think it's really cool; Moonshine is very lucky to have friends like you two. Bump sighed, pleased for them, and for Moonshine, but feeling a little sad for herself now that she didn't have her own girls that she could talk to every day.

"Well we could be your friends too if you wanted?" said Chloe who had started to play with her hair. Bump couldn't believe her ears for the second time that day.

Really? You would be my friends too?

Bump was at the door now and slowly pushed her head out through the opening. The two girls wasted no time in stroking her and rubbing her underneath her chin. Bump loved to be rubbed underneath her chin.

"Yes of course we will, you are the cutest little horse I think we have ever seen," said Amelia, tag-teaming with her sister now. "What's your name?"

Suddenly Bump felt really self-conscious; she didn't want to put her two new friends off, but when they saw her lumpy head she knew that they would probably just run away like most of the other children did. So this was a huge moment for her. She swallowed hard.

My name is Bump – or that's what I've always been called anyway. If you feel beneath my forelock, you will find out why.

With that she lowered her head, closed her eyes, and hoped that the two little girls wouldn't laugh at her.

Amelia was first to explore, rubbing Bump on her nose and then in between her eyes before reaching further up. Chloe watched her intently, happy for Amelia to be first but desperate to find out for herself what made this little horse so seemingly special.

Amelia suddenly stopped. Her eyes widened, and then a broad smile began to spread across her face.

"Wowwww, Chloe look at this!" and with that Amelia carefully parted the horse's forelock to reveal the lump to Chloe. Both girls gasped, but not in fear or ridicule but in awe; they looked at each other, smiled and then in unison squealed out loud:

"You've got a unicorn bump!"

Bump was flabbergasted.

A unicorn bump? But I'm a horse, not a unicorn!

"Well trust us, we love unicorns, and that is definitely a unicorn bump; they are really rare you know, but I've read all about them," explained Amelia, so excited to be talking to an actual unicorn horse.

Just then a grown-up's voice bellowed across the yard.

"Amelia Rose, Chloe Louise, come here right this instant!"

Oh dear, that grown-up doesn't look very happy, Bump thought.

"Ohhh don't worry it's only our mum, but we are sooo going to be in trouble now Chloe!" grumbled Amelia, but the expression on her face wasn't really one of utter terror. In fact far from it, she looked quite cool about it all. Bump was less calm though.

You must go, I've got you into trouble, I am so sorry!

Her ears were pinned back now with concern as she looked over as the grown-up started to pace across the yard towards them all.

"Don't worry, we are always in trouble for something! We are best friends as well as sisters you see, we go everywhere and we do everything together, including getting into trouble," added Chloe, smiling and rolling her eyes in light-hearted mockery before adding: "Bye-bye, see you again soon, Bump!" And with that she hopped off the step and pirouetted her way over to the approaching woman, meeting her halfway across the yard, just as it started to rain again.

Amelia though stayed behind. She wanted to talk to Bump in private.

"I've got to go too, but I just wanted to say goodbye properly." And with that Amelia looked over towards her mother to make sure that she was still busy having a stern word with Chloe before she leant into the stable, parted Bump's forelock again and gave her unicorn bump a big wet kiss goodbye.

"There, I just wanted to show you how much I already love you!" Amelia looked into Bump's eyes, and there was a connection there; the little horse stared back and saw nothing but genuine kindness in Amelia's eyes.

Oh, thank you so much, you don't know how special that makes me feel! Bump thought, a small equine tear welling up in the side of her eye. She blinked it away.

"Well, you are special, so that's okay! Goodbye Bump, but we will see you again soon I promise." With that Amelia turned and started heading back towards the inevitable telling off from her mother.

As she turned though Amelia glimpsed something bright materialising in the sky out of the corner of her eye. She stopped and looked round.

Behind her, the late afternoon sun was just peeking through a gap in the clouds. Amelia looked back towards where her mum and Chloe were standing; the sky above them was still a menacing dark grey loaded with rain, but as she looked up above their heads, her mouth fell open in wonderment at what she saw.

Emerging in front of the clouds was the most beautiful thing that Amelia had ever witnessed, its colours shimmering and sparkling like angel dust. She stood and watched in awe as the coloured arcs of the rainbow deepened as if they were flowing, becoming brighter as the bow snaked its path across the sky.

"Chloe, Chloe – LOOK!" Amelia yelled, desperate for her sister to see it too before it disappeared. Chloe didn't understand at first and just held her hands up as if to say: 'what have I done now?' Amelia pointed, Chloe turned, and then she saw it. She turned back towards Amelia, her face beaming as a smile erupted across it, and Amelia could see Chloe mouthing the word *wwwoooooowwww.*

Amelia was about to run over towards her sister, but instead she stopped and doubled back towards the stable.

Oh, you're back, what is it? Bump thought, pleased to see Amelia but puzzled to know what her newfound friend had come back for.

"LOOK!" Amelia gasped and pointed to the sky.

Bump strained her neck to look up and was instantly spellbound: she had never seen a rainbow before. Suddenly her head started to spin and throb in a whirl of colours and magical thoughts, it was as if all of the best things in the whole wide world were suddenly trying to get into her little head. The sensation made her feel all tingly and dreamy; she looked up again towards the sky and gazed at the rainbow which seemed to have become even brighter now.

"Do you like it?" Amelia asked. "Rainbows are rare and beautiful and very special – just like you!"

Bump didn't know what to think at first, but soon composed herself:

I LOVE it! It is beautiful, you're right, THANK YOU!

She pushed her head over the stable door and nuzzled into Amelia's shoulder, so eager to show her new friend how much she appreciated her that she nearly knocked her over.

"Hey, watch out! You nearly nuzzled me off my feet then!" squealed Amelia, not bothered at all by the thought. "I really have got to go now, or I will be in BIG trouble, my dad can get a bit grumpy sometimes so I don't want to spoil our first day here." She leant in and stroked Bump's head again before she left and said: "Goodbye Bump, our very own little unicorn horse!"

Up above, the rainbow faded as quickly and as quietly as it had manifested, its magic spell having already been cast.

It wasn't long afterwards that one of the stable hands came and closed Bump's stable up for the night; Bump lay down and was more than comfortable in her straw bed, but she couldn't stop thinking about Amelia and Chloe and all that had just happened. After so many years of wanting her own special little friend, suddenly she had two! Chloe had been the one that had found her, and Amelia had shown her the most magical thing that she had ever seen; and at that moment she knew that she was going to love her two new friends forever.

As she started to fall asleep Bump thought that she could feel a bit of a headache coming on, but she put it down to all the excitement from earlier. Before long she was soundly asleep imagining that she had a tail made up of all the colours of the rainbow and wings like an eagle so that she could soar high up into the sky, just as the rainbow had stretch out high above her earlier, dreaming that maybe one day she would be able to fly her new best friends all the way to the world where rainbows were made for lots of fun and new adventures...

Back at their new home Amelia and Chloe were thinking about rainbows too.

The new house was bigger than their old one and Chloe now had her own room, so they wouldn't be able to sit up all night talking about the magic as they usually did. At least each of them could fall asleep and dream whenever and about whatever they wanted to now. It didn't take long.

Both girls had thought of nothing other than going back to see Bump just as soon as they could. Once their mother had calmed down she had told them that since it was the summer holidays, they could go with her in the morning to make sure Moonshine was okay, providing that they behaved this time and didn't go running off again. Both girls had crossed their fingers behind their backs and promised that of course they wouldn't just go wandering off, and that they were sorry about earlier.

Sleep finally engulfed them both as they drifted off into dreams about rainbows and unicorns and lots of adventures, both girls the most excited they had been for a long time.

The sound of the birds singing their beautiful dawn chorus was the first thing that Chloe heard the following morning. She looked at her alarm clock: it was 7.14 am. She then crept through to Amelia's room; Amelia was already awake, and within ten more minutes, so was the rest of the household. Even Maxwell, their enormous, big-pawed tabby cat would have preferred a lie-in that morning, given all the upheaval and moving the previous day. By 8.00 am the two girls had showered, changed and had eaten breakfast, much to their mother Gillian's surprise.

The stables were only a seven or eight minute drive from the new house, and that morning it was even less given the early hour. They pulled in through the gate of the Mere Green Stable Yard and straight into a parking bay. The night before the whole place had seemed so busy, which Gillian thought was nice as it meant they had made a good choice for where to stable Moonshine.

Once parked they headed straight for the stable, all three eager to see how Moonshine had coped with his first night in his new home. Then Gillian remembered something that she had left in the car, and with annoyance told the girls to 'stay here and don't walk off' while she went back to fetch it.

Amelia looked at Chloe, and Chloe looked at Amelia who could tell exactly what her sister was thinking: 'let's run and see Bump!' Amelia knew that such a move would be way too risky though.

"Look, if we run off now, that's it. Mum will never let us explore again. So, let's just pretend we've been good girls and that we've done as we were told for a change, and then we might get a bit more freedom." Reluctantly, Chloe agreed.

Gillian soon returned from the car holding a black carrier bag, looking very excited. She met Amelia and Chloe and they walked round to see Moonshine in his new home. Neither of the girls knew what was in the bag but they didn't really care, all they could think about was how to escape to go and see Bump.

As they headed towards Moonshine's stable, Mrs Mullen came over to them and asked if she could speak to Gillian at some point whilst she was there, just to sign the paperwork and finalise the yard fees. Amelia immediately seized the opportunity.

"Mum, we will be okay if you need to go and sort things out; we can go and find out where everything is and where we need to go for things if you like?" She added an angelic smile just to seal the deal.

"Well, alright but don't go far; any more repeats of yesterday and you won't be coming again, is that understood?" Chloe and Amelia both nodded 'yes Mum'. Result. "OKAY but I need your help first." Not so good.

"Awww Mum, wot?" It was Amelia's resolve that cracked first.

"Don't 'wot' me young lady; I wanted you to see this." with which

Moonshine

she pulled a slate plaque out of the carrier bag and held it up in front of the two girls. Painted on it in luminescent white paint was the word 'Moonshine'

"It looks amazing!" said Amelia, genuinely impressed. Chloe agreed, all the while imagining a similar plaque for Bump, each letter a different colour of the rainbow and with a unicorn flying over the capital 'B'.

"Can we go and start finding out where things are now please Mum?" asked Amelia hopefully.

"Yes, off you go then but don't be long now. You have thirty minutes that's all, is that understood? Meet me back here, I want to put the plaque up before we go."

The girls shouted 'okaaaaaay' as they slowly walked off, looking as though they didn't know where they were heading. Of course, they knew *exactly* where they were heading.

They risked one glance round to make sure their mum was already preoccupied; when they saw her laughing and chatting with Mrs Mullen they knew that they were in the clear, and their slow steps turning into a much quicker skip across the yard towards where Bump's stable was.

Bump had awoken that Friday morning with the strangest feeling inside her.

Her head felt heavy as if she had been eating apples that had gone off the night before. She knew she hadn't, but she thought that's what it must feel like.

She looked around her stable: nothing had changed. Maybe she had just had a bad dream and hadn't slept for as long as she thought. She shook her head to try and clear the feeling, but that only seemed to make things worse. Her head felt ever so heavy. *How very strange*, she thought to herself.

Just then she heard footsteps, followed by the unmistakable voices of her two new human friends Amelia and Chloe. She instantly felt better. She had wondered if she had just imagined everything that had happened the day before, but now Bump knew that she hadn't. She trotted over towards the stable door which had been unbolted, although the top hatch hadn't been opened yet, and waited patiently for Amelia and Chloe to arrive.

The two girls approached the stable with such excitement; when they saw that the top door was still closed, however, they didn't know what to do.

"Shall we just open it?" asked Chloe, holding out both her hands in a 'it won't hurt' gesture.

Bump heard what Chloe had said and thought as loud as she could: *yes, it's open, just pull the handle and secure the latch the other side,* but she knew that the girls were probably too far away for them to hear what she had thought... She hoofed at the stable floor and whinnied out loud in frustration.

Just then Maria appeared across the yard.

"It's okay, just open it and secure the latch, I will be over to feed her in a bit," Maria called out, recognising the two girls from the day before.

"Okay thanks!" called back Amelia, Chloe waving at her as she headed for the main stable complex pushing a wheelbarrow crammed full of bags of juicy carrots.

"Pass me the step Chloe." Chloe obliged. Amelia then stepped up and grabbed the handle on the top stable door.

Bump pricked up her ears when she heard them, she couldn't believe that she was going to see them again so soon. She edged closer to the stable door.

Amelia pulled the handle, and the door slowly but surely swung open to let the daylight in and to allow Bump to look out. However, as the door swung across the front of the stable, both Amelia and Chloe's faces changed when they saw what stood in front of them.

"Oh...My...GOODNESS!!!" exclaimed Amelia.

"OH WOWWWWWWWW, that is so COOOOLLLLL!" whooped Chloe, bouncing up and down and clapping her hands together in front of her face.

What, what's wrong? thought Bump; she was still inside the stable, but without realising it she had edged close enough now for the girls to hear what she was thinking.

Amelia looked at Chloe, who just stared at Bump, open mouthed. Neither girl could speak. Eventually Chloe tried.

"You-are-a-UNICORN!"

Sitting proudly on top of Bump's forehead was the most amazing and most unique unicorn horn that the two girls could have ever imagined, its bright ivory spiral sparkling in the early morning sunlight.

I'm a – what?! thought Bump. She presumed that she must have misheard Chloe, because how on earth could she just turn into a unicorn – that was impossible!

"Bump, I can't believe I am about to say this," exclaimed Amelia, "but – you *do* appear to have become a unicorn – or at least you have a unicorn's horn!"

Bump was dumbfounded. She wished she could see what all the fuss was about for herself. Luckily Amelia heard her think it.

"Wait there," Amelia said and jumped down from the step and ran off towards the main stable block.

Two minutes later she returned with a big yellow horse ball that had a mirror embedded into one side.

"What's that?" asked Chloe.

"I saw it this morning, I am sure the horse who it belongs to won't mind if we borrow it for a minute! Look Bump," and with that Amelia held the toy up in front of the puzzled little horse's face.

Bump had never seen herself before.

She looked in amazement as Amelia slowly raised the mirrored ball up and down in front of her so that she could see the horn in all its glory for herself.

Oh my, well that's a little odd isn't it! was all that Bump could think to think.

A little odd?" laughed Amelia. "It's more than a little odd, it's absolutely unbelievable!" Chloe nodded in agreement, her face still beaming and unable to take her eyes off the horn that now proudly adorned the horses head.

Bump started to wiggle her head around, trying to get used to the strange new weight of her unicorn horn. After a bit of to-ing and fro-ing she seemed to get the hang of it and proceeded to gambol around the stable, causing Amelia and Chloe to laugh and squeal along with her.

"How do you feel?" Chloe asked eventually.

I feel great, especially now I know I've got a unicorn horn! I woke up feeling a little different this morning, but I just presumed it was because I was tired, Bump thought, trying to piece together everything that had happened in the last twenty-four hours.

Last night when you came back to say goodnight properly Amelia I felt a bit strange, like I was in a dream, especially when I saw that magical rainbow. Then before I fell asleep, I had a slight headache. I guess whatever happened must have caused my horn to grow!

Suddenly the girls heard footsteps behind them. It was their mum and she didn't look at all happy.

Amelia and Chloe instinctively bunched close together on the step to try and hide Bump from view.

"Right girls that's it, I warned you earlier, I've been waiting for ov..." Her words trailed off.

In front of her, Gillian watched in disbelief as a beautiful ivory horn popped out of the stable doorway between her two daughters. Attached to the horn was a little white horse with a messy black forelock. Gillian looked at Amelia and Chloe, and her daughters looked back at their mum, trembling.

Uh-oh, thought Bump.

"'Uh-oh' indeed!" said Gillian, her hands on her hips trying to look as angry as she could without smiling at the look of utter shock that suddenly spreading across the girls faces.

"HUH?" said Amelia and Chloe in unison again. Gillian kept her stern surprised look going for as long as she could, until she couldn't help but smile.

"What, you didn't both think that you were the only ones who can hear what animals are thinking, did you?" and with that Gillian smiled and went over to the stable, instinctively putting one arm around each of the confused girls' shoulders. Then she looked at Bump.

"And I never thought I'd ever see one like you again, little horse," she said and leaned across and stroked Bump gently on the nose. Now Bump was really confused.

So you can hear me too? My thoughts I mean, you can hear my thoughts? But you are a grown-up! Bump thought, her head starting to spin again now.

"Yes, but I was a little girl too you know, once upon a time." Gillian smiled, a knowing smile.

"So, you knew that we could talk to Charlie? And Maxwell – and Moonshine? And you never thought to say anything?" Amelia was a little cross – she couldn't quite believe that her mother had the magic too and that she had never told them.

"Yes, I used to listen to you both talking to Charlie, and then I would go and ask Charlie if you were okay once you'd gone off to do whatever it was you were going to do. Just to be sure. I do the same with Maxwell now. So be warned girls, think about what you tell your cat in future!"

Gillian couldn't resist the last bit, although she had never really asked Maxwell about what secrets her girls had chosen to share with him. She didn't need to.

What did you mean when you said that you never thought you'd see one of 'me' again? Bump thought, desperate to know now if she was truly unique or if there were other unicorn horses out there somewhere. Gillian stroked Bump's face lovingly as she explained.

"When I was a little girl I lived on a farm in Cayderwood; the people who owned the farmhouse next door were a lovely old couple, Mr and Mrs Dingle, who always said hello but kept themselves to themselves. Sometimes I used to watch them from my bedroom window." Gillian looked down at the floor and started kicking the dirt with her foot as she began to recall events that had been locked away inside her for many years. "I noticed that sometimes they used to walk out of the back of their garden and along a track to what looked like a wooden hut just inside the forest. I always wondered what they were going there to do, and who – or what – they were going to see." Gillian paused and looked up to see that she now had three pairs of eyes staring at her, hanging on her every word.

"So one day I went and had a look."

"Wow, did you break into the hut?" asked Chloe, her young rebellious mind swirling as she imagined all the things that could live in a secret hut in the middle of a forest.

"No, of course not; I waited until I knew they were out, and then I squeezed through a gap in the hedge at the bottom of the field where our two gardens bordered one another. Then I went to see what I could see through the windows."

"What was in there?" It was Amelia's turn now, already imagining a goblin, a troll or a dragon or something being held captive.

"It was a little unicorn horse. just like you, er…"

"Bump, her name is Bump and I found her!" proclaimed Chloe, eager to assert ownership rights over their magic little unicorn horse.

"Oh, well hello, Bump, I am very pleased to meet you," with which Gillian stroked Bump's mane and rubbed her under her chin.

"So what happened to your unicorn horse, Mum?" asked Amelia.

"I don't know; we had to move away. They called her Rosy because she always had rosy cheeks after she had been running around in the paddock for a while, she told me that day. That's when I realised that I had the magic too. Anyway, I tried to go and see Rosy the day we left but we were late, and I didn't get chance; I'm sure she is still running around though just as happy!" Gillian's discomfort was eased when from behind her Mrs Mullen called out, indicating that she needed to see her again. Luckily, she hadn't come too close and so she couldn't see Bump.

"So, are you going to tell anyone?" Chloe asked, scared now that someone would want to steal Bump from them.

"No of course not but you can't hide Bump away in here forever." Then she looked at Bump.

"As for you Bump, you will have to show everybody at some point won't you!"

But what if they laugh at me? Bump thought nervously.

"I bet they don't. You wait and see." and with that Gillian kissed Amelia and Chloe on their heads, stroked Bump on her forelock and headed back towards Mrs Mullen. She knew that the girls would want to stay with Bump now but it didn't matter, because now that she knew where they were and what they were doing, she was happy. Just to be sure though, she went back to see Moonshine and asked him to keep his beady eyes on them, to which he nodded his head three times in agreement before gratefully accepting the carrot that Gillian had for him.

The only other person to come near to Bump's stable that day was Maria, and with the girls help Bump managed to hide her unicorn horn in a hay net while Maria replenished her bedding. After that Bump and the two girls spent ages wondering what to do next, and as usual, the two girls had slightly different opinions.

"No, do it today!" whined Chloe, the 'it' in question being whether

Bump should parade herself around that day, or the following weekend. Amelia, ever the deeper thinking of the two sisters disagreed.

"Look, I reckon we are better off doing it tomorrow. It's the weekend and there will be loads more people here; it just makes more sense!" Then, thinking on her feet, Amelia added, "And Chloe, if there are more people here, there will be more children here, and they will all see Bump with us, and then they will all want to be our friends, because who wouldn't want to be friends with the two new girls whose best friend was a unicorn horse, huh?" Chloe thought about it and then smiled.

"Yeah, that would be kind of cool!" and with that, the two girls sat down in the hay with Bump and hatched the most exciting plan ever.

The following day turned out to be truly magical.

Amelia and Chloe arrived at the stables early that morning and spent ages brushing Bump's coat, and then even longer combing Bump's tail and frizzy mane. Chloe then managed to plait Bump's mane into lots of neat little bundles, then polished and shined Bump's hooves before adding the final touches that they had discussed the evening before.

At midday they opened Bump's stable gate and led Bump out into the yard and over towards the main stable block, all the time looking at each other, looking back at Bump and smiling at the thought of what was about to happen.

It was Maria who was the first person to see them, and she promptly dropped the bucket of horse manure that she was carrying. Then Mrs Mullen saw them out of her office window, and she proceeded to pour her mug of tea all down her front and all over her computer.

Veronica Mullen had just walked out of the office into the yard when she had turned to see what all the fuss was about, and with eyes like saucers she just carried on walking – straight into the open stable door opposite, tripping over a bucket and falling into a trough of cold water.

The first child to see Bump was Millie Tucker; all she could say was "Is that a..." before fainting into Gracie Meadows' arms. Gracie herself then proceeded to wet herself and immediately ran off towards her mother screaming, "I want a unicorn horse too Mother, it's so unfair!"

Cassie was at the yard that day; when she saw Bump, she smiled to herself, amazed at how magnificent she looked; she'd always known that the little horse was different. Bump saw her and stopped, keen to say thank you to the only friend she'd had for such a long time for being so kind to her; Cassie knew what Bump was thinking, although she had never let on, and she felt happy tears well up inside her at the thought that the little horse was no longer alone.

To be fair, Bump did look amazing.

Her coat shimmered and her hooves glistened in the morning sun as her mane bounced from side to side, her tail swishing with pride as she cantered through the growing crowds, whinnying and neighing her little horsey sounds as she went. She stopped every time she was asked to, bowed her head, and let everyone touch the beautiful spiral centrepiece that adorned the top of her head.

Everyone she met simply adored her that day; even the children that had previously made fun of her. She didn't mind though. Bump didn't believe in bearing grudges, because after all, life was too short for all that nonsense.

Anyway, gone now was the lump that had been the reason that so many people had been so mean to her in the past. She was no longer the ugly duckling. In its place sat a single spiral horn

standing proud and tall, decked out like a magnificent totem pole adorned with seven coloured balloons bouncing on the breeze, each one tied on in the order of the colours of the rainbow from top to bottom: Red, Orange, Yellow, Green, Blue, Indigo and Violet.

The highlight for Bump, though, was when she reached the fields.

The first two horses that greeted her were Shire and Bodo; both instantly came across and told her how wonderful she looked. Then Sky bounded over with Thelma in close pursuit, and when Thelma saw Bump, she merely lowered her head in acknowledgement and whispered, 'you look stunning my dear,' any previous animosity she might have felt disappearing in an instant. 'Sky then proceeded to go galloping around the field like a mad thing, ending up in a puddle of mud which delighted her, although Thelma hadn't looked quite so pleased.

As Bump cantered around the field, more and more horses trotted over to see her and to admire her fantastic unicorn horn. None of the other mares had ever seen an *actual* unicorn horse before; a lot of the fillies could remember dreaming about growing up to be a unicorn one day, and now, one of their own had done it.

From that day on, Bump knew that she would live happily ever after.

The following week Veronica Mullen moved Bump into the stable next to Moonshine, the day after Gracie Meadows' horse Otto's sudden departure from the yard. Gracie's mother Penelope had stated that her reason for leaving was nothing to do with the little problem that Gracie had experienced the previous week, because 'after all it could happen to any twelve-year-old'... instead it was because she didn't want her precious little daughter to have to mix with the common hoi polloi that she said would be descending on the 'grubby little stables' now to look at the 'ghastly little rainbow horse'. Gracie Meadows never did get her own unicorn horse though.

Moonshine and Bump hadn't minded; they loved living next door to each other, and they had soon become the best of horsey friends, although Bump would never be able to tell Moonshine just how much she liked him. *He was just sooo gorgeous,* she thought to herself on a daily basis, just far enough away so that Moonshine couldn't hear her thoughts.

Later that summer, Bump was asked to go to a local hospital to meet the children that were staying there. The looks on their faces when they saw her would live with her forever, and Bump finally realised that she was now able to give a little of her magic back to the world.

To Bump, that made her feel happier than any magic spell that any wizard could ever cast, anywhere in the universe...

She became the star attraction at the Mere Green Stable Yard, often having her photograph taken for the national newspapers amidst a worldwide fascination for a real-life unicorn. She even made it onto the front page of Horse & Hound one month alongside the headline: 'Bump: The magical little unicorn horse'.

She took it all at a canter though.

Best of all was that she could spend as much time as she liked and she could go wherever she wanted with her two favourite humans, and they spent all their spare time together that summer playing and dreaming of the adventures that they could have, just Amelia, Chloe and Bump.

And, thought Bump, guess what: all of those adventures might well come to life one day, just you wait and see... and just imagine what fun we could all have if I was to grow wings too...

Just imagine that.

HOSPITAL

THE END.